I AM A GOOD DIGITAL CITIZEN

I AM
RESPECTFUL
ONLINE

RACHAEL MORLOCK

PowerKiDS press

NEW YORK

Published in 2020 by The Rosen Publishing Group, Inc.
29 East 21st Street, New York, NY 10010

Copyright © 2020 by The Rosen Publishing Group, Inc.

All rights reserved. No part of this book may be reproduced in any form without permission in writing from the publisher, except by a reviewer.

First Edition

Editor: Elizabeth Krajnik
Book Design: Reann Nye

Photo Credits: Cover, pp. 5 wavebreakmedia/Shutterstock.com; p. 7 Twin Design/Shutterstock.com; p. 9 Robert Kneschke/Shutterstock.com; pp. 11, 13 Hero Images/Getty Images; p. 15 Flashpop/DigitalVision/Getty Images; p. 17 Samuel Borges Photography/Shutterstock.com; p. 19 Syda Productions/Shutterstock.com; p. 21 Fascinadora/Shutterstock.com; p. 22 Lopolo/Shutterstock.com.

Cataloging-in-Publication Data

Names: Morlock, Rachael.
Title: I am respectful online / Rachael Morlock.
Description: New York : PowerKids Press, 2020. | Series: I am a good digital citizen | Includes glossary and index.
Identifiers: ISBN 9781538349649 (pbk.) | ISBN 9781538349663 (library bound) | ISBN 9781538349656 (6pack)
Subjects: LCSH: Online etiquette–Juvenile literature. | Internet–Moral and ethical aspects–Juvenile literature. | Internet and children–Juvenile literature.
Classification: LCC TK5105.878 M673 2020 | DDC 004.67'80835–dc23

Manufactured in the United States of America

CPSIA Compliance Information: Batch #CSPK19. For Further Information contact Rosen Publishing, New York, New York at 1-800-237-9932.

CONTENTS

DOING YOUR DUTY 4
SHOWING RESPECT 6
RESPECT PEOPLE 8
RESPECT OPINIONS 10
RESPECT PRIVACY 12
ASK FOR PERMISSION 14
SHARING ONLINE 16
GIVING CREDIT 18
HOW TO GIVE CREDIT 20
SAFE AND FRIENDLY 22
GLOSSARY 23
INDEX 24
WEBSITES 24

DOING YOUR DUTY

The Internet connects a huge community of people around the world. Going on the Internet on a phone, tablet, or computer is like stepping into a large public place. It's a place where you can play, learn, and make friends. While you're online, it's your duty to be a good digital citizen.

SHOWING RESPECT

You can be a good digital citizen by following rules, staying safe, and showing kindness and respect when connecting with others. Showing respect is about treating others well. You show respect when you let others be themselves. Honoring the **privacy** and the creations of others are also ways to act with respect.

RESPECT PEOPLE

Did you know that about half of the world's **population** uses the Internet? It's important to respect everyone you meet online, no matter who or where they are. You can respect people who look, think, and act differently than you by being kind and **polite** online.

RESPECT OPINIONS

You won't agree with everything you read and see online—that's OK! The Internet is large enough to hold many **opinions** at one time. You can disagree in a polite way. Choose your words carefully and consider other peoples' respectful views. You might learn to see things in a new way!

RESPECT PRIVACY

Another important job for digital citizens is to respect the privacy of others. Digital **devices**, including phones, tablets, and computers, often hold peoples' private **information**. Always ask before using another person's device. Help them guard their important information. You can honor others' privacy by only using your own accounts and devices.

ASK FOR PERMISSION

Asking for **permission** is an easy way to show respect. You and your friends might have different safety and privacy rules. Always ask before you share information, photos, or messages that include other people. If you'd like to post a picture of yourself with your best friends, ask them if it's OK first!

SHARING ONLINE

Have you ever found words, pictures, ideas, or information online that you really liked? If you're **excited** about something new, it's natural to want to share it. But you shouldn't copy or steal from others. Before you borrow things online, ask permission of the creator. If they say no, don't borrow it!

GIVING CREDIT

Once you have permission to borrow something, make sure you give credit when using it. That means telling others where you found ideas, pictures, or information on the Internet. If you didn't create it, giving credit to the creator is the respectful thing to do. Then you can share the fun, helpful things you find online.

HOW TO GIVE CREDIT

If you use the Internet for help doing homework, you must give credit for the information and ideas you find. A website's online address, or URL, usually starts with "www." Naming this address is one way to give credit. That makes it easy for your teacher and other students to find the **sources** you used.

21

SAFE AND FRIENDLY

Respect is necessary for healthy friendships—online and offline. It allows you to make positive connections with people. It helps you guard the privacy of others. It guides you in giving credit where credit is due. With respect, the Internet becomes a safer and friendlier place for **interacting** with others.

GLOSSARY

device: A tool used for a certain purpose.

excited: Feeling or showing a great amount of interest.

information: Knowledge or facts about something.

interact: To act together.

opinion: A judgment or belief.

permission: The approval of a person in charge.

polite: Showing courtesy or good manners.

population: The number of people who live in a place.

privacy: The quality of being away from public attention.

source: A person, place, or thing from which something comes or where it can be found.

INDEX

A
accounts, 12

C
computer, 4, 12
creator, 16, 18
credit, 18, 20, 22

D
devices, 12

F
friends, 4, 14, 22

I
information, 12, 14, 16, 18, 20
Internet, 4, 8, 18, 20, 22

K
kindness, 6

M
messages, 14

O
opinions, 10

P
permission, 14, 16, 18
phone, 4, 12
photos, 14
pictures, 14, 16, 18
privacy, 6, 12, 14, 22

R
rules, 6, 14

T
tablet, 4, 12

V
views, 10

W
website, 20
words, 10, 16

WEBSITES

Due to the changing nature of Internet links, PowerKids Press has developed an online list of websites related to the subject of this book. This site is updated regularly. Please use this link to access the list: www.powerkidslinks.com/digcit/respectful

TITLES IN THIS SERIES

I AM ALERT ONLINE

I AM BRAVE ONLINE

I AM COURTEOUS ONLINE

I AM KIND ONLINE

I AM RESPECTFUL ONLINE

I AM SMART ONLINE

I AM STRONG ONLINE

GRL: K

ISBN: 9781538349649
6-pack ISBN: 9781538349656

PowerKiDS press